MARIA
MONTOYA MARTINEZ
MASTER POTTER

MARIA
MONTOYA MARTINEZ
MASTER POTTER

Especially for Peggy!
Elsie Karr Kreischer

Elsie Karr Kreischer

Illustrated by
Elsie Karr Kreischer
and Roberta Sinnock

PELICAN PUBLISHING COMPANY
Gretna 1995

*The word "Pelican" and the depiction of a pelican are trademarks
of Pelican Publishing Company, Inc.,
and are registered in the U.S. Patent and Trademark Office.*

Library of Congress Cataloging-in-Publication Data

Kreischer, Elsie Karr.
    María Montoya Martínez, master potter / by Elsie Karr
Kreischer ; illustrated by Elsie Karr Kreischer and Roberta
Sinnock.
      p. cm.
    ISBN 1-56554-098-0
    1. Martínez, María Montoya—Juvenile literature. 2. Tewa
women—New Mexico—San Ildefonso—Biography—Juvenile liter-
ature. 3. Potters—New Mexico—San Ildefonso—Biography—Juve-
nile literature. 4. Tewa pottery—New Mexico—San Ildefonso—
Biography—Juvenile literature. 5. San Ildefonso (N.M.)—Biogra-
phy—Juvenile literature. [1. Martínez, María Montoya. 2. Pueblo
Indians—Biography. 3. Indians of North America—New Mexico—
Biography. 4. Women—Biography. 5. Artists.] I. Sinnock, Roberta,
ill. II. Title.
E99.S213.M3746 1995
738'.092—dc20
[B]   95-8198
                                          CIP
                                          AC

Manufactured in the United States of America

Published by Pelican Publishing Company, Inc.
1101 Monroe Street, Gretna, Louisiana 70053

*To Edna Norton, who opened the door,
and to Adam and Santana, who kept it open*

The old cottonwood tree in the middle of María's village plaza

In memory of Alice Marriott,
who planned to write the foreword for this book.
Unfortunately, like María and Old Grandmother,
she went away before it was finished.

Contents

Acknowledgments

I wish to offer my special thanks to the University of Oklahoma for permission to use parts of Alice Marriott's book, *María: The Potter of San Ildefonso;* to Richard L. Spivey for his expertise; to Joe S. Sando, Pueblo Historian; to Dr. Jeanne Whitehouse; and to my longtime writing friends of the Albuquerque Society for Children's Book Writers and Illustrators. Without their help and encouragement this book would not have been written.

Introduction

An old-timer once said that María Montoya Martínez, pottery maker, was the only queen that America ever had. María never lived like royalty. She was born in 1887 at the San Ildefonso Indian pueblo, which is a village near Santa Fe in New Mexico. She lived in a warm adobe house with her family.

Like all little girls, María played with mud or clay. While most of them made "mud pies," María made pots. Her playing grew into an immense love for clay, which she developed into the craft of pottery making. Through that craft she came to be considered as the most outstanding Indian artist of all time. She won so many awards for her work that some were lost or forgotten.

The awards María received were not important to her. Caring for her people meant more. She shared her knowledge and her money with them. She wanted everyone to be equal.

María's life was not easy. Making pots was hard work but she never gave up. She wanted to make pots that were as good as Old Grandmother's and Tía Nicolasa's. And she did. Hers were even better.

María's work and caring gave her the qualities of a queen even though she never lived in a castle.

CHAPTER ONE

The Spotted Sickness

A fierce wind shrieked over the mesa, blasting the courtyard with stinging sand. Like crazed demons, tumble-
weeds spun across the plaza, scratching eerily as they
slammed against the windows at the San Ildefonso Indian
pueblo near Santa Fe in New Mexico.

Inside her warm adobe home, ten-year-old María was
not aware of the storm as she lay on her shelf-bed along
the wall. Nor was she conscious of the two women caring
for her. As the storm raged on, shaking the house and rat-
tling the windows, the women paid it no attention. They
were battling a storm of their own: María's illness.

For two days, Mother and Tía Nicolasa watched
María's pox-marked body as her life ebbed away. They
cried silently as María grew weaker and no longer
responded to their voices.

"I'll get some herb tea," Tía Nicolasa said, going to the
kitchen. "It's the only medicine we have."

While Mother waited for the tea she knelt by María
and prayed: "Hail Mary, full of grace . . ."

"Drink this, María," Mother coaxed, when Tía Nicolasa
returned. "It will help you." She pulled gently at María's
lips. They would not open. They were too swollen and

covered with smallpox scabs to move. Finally Mother managed to part them slightly.

Tía Nicolasa trickled the sacred herbs over María's lips but the liquid just spilled down her chin. Discouraged, Tía Nicolasa took the herbs away and came back with a basin of cool water. "I think we should bathe her," she said, handing the basin to Mother. "She's burning up with fever."

María lay as still as a stick while the women bathed her. She never opened her eyes nor did she move in any way. It was as if she didn't care what they did.

At first the water cooled her. Then suddenly, as the storm grew fiercer, her fever climbed higher. Quietly, she slipped into a coma.

"That's all we can do," Mother said. "It's out of our hands." Pulling her shawl over her head, she sat down near the fireplace. Tía Nicolasa shook her head sadly and sat down beside her.

They stopped speaking and prayed. They knew that three more people in San Ildefonso had died. As their hands moved wearily over their rosaries they wondered if María would be next.

The night dragged on as the storm continued to batter the house. Exhausted, worried, and helpless, the women dozed. From time to time they awakened to check on María. They found no change. María was as helpless against the *spotted sickness* (smallpox) as the house was against the fury of the storm.

Hours later María cried out. "Oh-o-o-o, Oh-o-o-o," she moaned. Her voice wavered with pain.

Startled, the women looked at one another in disbelief. They hurried to María's side, knowing she was worse. Mother looked at her and placed her hand over María's pox-marked brow.

"Is she dying?" whispered Tía Nicolasa.

"María," Mother cried, ignoring Tía Nicolasa. "Can you hear me?"

María moaned softly. "Oh-o-o-o."

"Let's bathe her again," Tía Nicolasa said, but Mother shook her head and glanced at the fireplace. There were a few embers in it—just right for what she had in mind.

"Let's smoke her," she whispered. "I heard it helped an old man down near the river."

Tía Nicolasa nodded. Pulling her shawl closer, she started out the door. A strong gust of wind slammed her back against the house. She hesitated a second, then gathering her strength, pushed her way into the swirling debris of the storm.

A few minutes later she made her way back into the house with an armload of green cedar boughs. Carefully she placed some of them on the hot embers, where they blazed into a fire. Each time it blazed she smothered the flames with more branches. Soon smoke billowed out into the room. The thicker it became, the more branches she piled on the smoldering coals, creating a strong piney odor.

Finally satisfied that there was enough smoke in the room, the women waved it toward María with their shawls. Tía Nicolasa kept waving the smoke and Mother knelt beside María again. "Santo Niño," she prayed to the children's saint. "Please let María live. If she lives I will send her on a pilgrimage to you. She will thank you, Santo Niño. I promise."

María shivered. She could hear her mother's voice. It was like placing her hand on a drum with her ears closed—although she couldn't hear the drum, its vibrations would surge first through her fingers, up her arms, and then throughout her body. It was a scary feeling.

She didn't know what Mother was saying but she knew that it was important. She wanted to see Mother. She struggled to open her eyes. But they were stuck tight. They were too heavy with smallpox scabs. They felt itchy. She itched all over and the scabs hurt.

I smell smoke, she thought, trying to twitch her nose. *Cedar smoke.*

Just then a strong gust of smoke hit her in the face. It filled her nostrils and sprayed her lungs. She began to choke. Coughing and spitting, she gasped for air. Tears spilled out of her eyes. They ran down her cheeks in little crooked paths around the scabs.

"María!" Mother cried. "Are you all right?"

María heard Mother's words but she could not answer. Her throat was too sore. She wanted to see Mother. Mother would make her well.

She tried to open her eyes. They would not open. She pushed and strained until they opened a tiny crack.

I see Mother, she cried inwardly. *I see her! But Mother doesn't know that I see her.*

I'm smiling, too, she thought, trying to move her lips. *I'm smiling on the inside, even though it hurts.* María knew Tía Nicolasa had brought a pot of healing herbs into the room. She had heard her tell Mother that they were fresh and warm.

Again, Mother pulled at María's lips as Tía Nicolasa let the liquid trickle slowly into her mouth. As they worked, María swallowed small sips of the liquid. She felt its soothing power as it ran down her throat. The herbs made her feel better.

The next morning the storm was spent and the sun rose high in the sky. María opened her eyes to happy smiles on the women's faces.

"Santo Niño answered my prayers," she heard Mother say as she put her shawl away.

Tía Nicolasa clasped Mother's hand and whispered, "Thanks be to God. María *will* live."

CHAPTER TWO

Poveka

A few weeks later María slipped through the back door. It was the first time she had been outside since the spotted sickness. She drew a deep breath and gazed at the bright turquoise sky.

The sky was the same color as the ring on her finger. The turquoise stone in the ring was for good luck. I had good luck, María thought. I didn't die. For a second she stared at the apple trees, then started running toward them. She had to stop. She was too weak to run. She must walk.

When she reached the trees she stood silently before them. Then she leaned her head against the biggest one. "I can feel you vibrating," she said. "Just like a drum." Rubbing her fingers over the rough bark she knew that they were one and the same . . . part of the great spirit. "I can still smell your apple blossoms," she whispered. "Even if they are all gone."

Mother had brought her apple blossoms when she was sick. She placed them in water to keep them alive. But they had died, just as all things do.

I didn't die, María thought, inhaling deeply. She smelled a rich fertile odor. It was a sharp aroma of earthen dampness. It was the same smell as when Father plowed the fields for planting. She didn't work in the fields like her

older sister, Ana. She just enjoyed walking in the freshly
plowed rows when she carried water for them to drink.

María loved her pueblo. She loved everything about it,
even the odor of wood smoke from the stoves and fire-
places. After all, it had saved her life.

For a moment she watched the smoke as it spiraled
upward over the pueblo, then walked on. Cutting through
the apple orchard she hurried past the playhouse near
the acequia, the irrigation ditch. She wanted to see something in the water—something important.

"María," Desidéria called, running after her. "Where
are you going?"

María paused. Then she continued walking along the
top of the ditch. She walked slowly as she looked down into
the shadowy water.

"María, come back!" Desidéria begged. "You know
Mother said not to go near the acequia."

María pretended not to hear her sister and walked on.
Finally finding what she was looking for, she stopped. She
stood silently by the water's edge, studying a patch of floating vines.

"There's a *poveka!*" she cried, pointing toward the
vines. "A yellow pond lily! Do you see it, Desidéria? Do you
see it?"

María reached for the lily. But she couldn't touch it. So
she stood quietly, watching it float in the water.

"You have a pretty name, Poveka," whispered Desidéria, slipping up behind her.

María was surprised to be called by her Indian name.
She turned to smile at her sister. The Indian name was
usually reserved for special occasions such as sacred
dances, weddings, or funerals.

"It's a nice custom for grandmothers to name a new
baby," Desidéria continued. "Grandmother gave you a nice
name."

María nodded, remembering the story. Grandmother

went for an early walk the morning María was born. The sun had just come up. The first thing she saw was the yellow pond lily. She named María for the bright flower she saw floating like a golden nugget in the sunlit water.

"I like it," María said, not taking her eyes off the lily. "When I have a little girl I will give her the same name."

"It will be a long time before you have a little girl," Desidéria said. "You'd better name your doll that first."

"No!" retorted María. "I can wait."

After prayers that night, Mother talked to María. She spoke in a low voice. She did not want Desidéria and Ana to hear what she was saying. It was a secret. María was pleased. Secrets were fun, even if they were hard to keep.

"María," Mother said softly. "When you had the *spotted sickness* I made a promise to Santo Niño. Now I must keep that promise."

María looked at her mother. She did not ask what the promise was. That would not have been polite. She wanted to know so much that little shivers ran up and down her back.

"I thought you were going to die," Mother said. "Tía Nicolasa thought so, too." Mother hesitated, then looked down at María. "We tried everything we knew to save you."

María smiled. She wished Mother would hurry and tell her the secret. What did she promise?

"I asked Santo Niño to let you live," Mother said. "That's when I made the promise."

María noticed a fine layer of moisture on Mother's brow. It looked as if she had been sweeping the plaza. *Talking isn't work,* María thought. *So why is she perspiring? Is it because of the secret?*

"I promised Santo Niño that if you lived you would go on a pilgrimage," Mother finally said. "A pilgrimage to thank him."

A pilgrimage? María shivered. A pilgrimage was important. That made her important.

"María, it's time for you to go," Mother continued. "You will go to Chimayo to thank Santo Niño."

"To Chimayo?" she questioned. "That's a long way from the pueblo. How will I get there?"

"You will walk," Mother said.

"I . . . will . . . walk?" María burst out.

"Shush. . . ." Mother placed her hand over María's mouth. "Remember our secret."

"Will I go tomorrow?" María whispered. Already she was thinking how important she was.

"No. You are still too weak," Mother said, pulling the blanket up around María's shoulders. "It's ten miles there. That is too far for you right now."

"Will I have fun on the pilgrimage?" María asked, anticipating a good time playing with her sisters.

Mother shook her head. "A pilgrimage is a serious thing. You must prepare for it."

"How?"

"You must pray."

"Are Desidéria and Ana going?" she asked. "And will they have to pray, too?"

"No," Mother said. "Only you will go. You were the one who was sick." She looked to see if the girls were asleep or if they had heard her talking to María. "Don't tell them yet. It must be kept a secret."

María giggled. Her hand flew over her mouth to muffle the sound. A secret, and only she would know!

"Shush . . .," Mother warned again, placing her fingers over her lips. "Shush. . . ."

María looked down at her blanket. She didn't want Mother to know what she was thinking. She wouldn't approve. Everyone was supposed to be the same. María thought she was special.

When Mother left the room, María tossed and turned. The more she thought about the secret, the bigger it became. *Desidéria and Ana will be mad,* she thought. *Mad because they don't know.* María could not go to sleep. All night long and the next day the secret kept playing hopscotch in her mind. It wanted out. It jumped from one place to another.

Finally, it grew so big that María almost burst. She knew she couldn't keep carrying it around. She must do something about it.

I won't tell, she thought, looking it straight in the eye. *I made a promise and I will keep it.* But keeping a secret, she decided as she watched her sisters play string games, is as hard as making small pots.

"It's even harder," she murmured, "than holding a little bird in your hand and keeping it from flying away."

CHAPTER THREE

The Pilgrimage

María thought about the secret constantly. It never left her for a moment. At times she had to bite her tongue to keep it from spilling out. The more she thought about it the more special she felt, even if it was wrong to feel that way.

One morning Mother scolded her. "You must think about something besides yourself, María. Think about Old Grandmother and your sisters. Think about your duties in the pueblo. We must all work together."

"How did Mother know what I was thinking?" María muttered to herself. "Only I know what I think." But Mother was right. She always knew what María had in mind.

"Get your broom, María," Mother called, going toward the courtyard. "It's time to sweep the plaza. You may play later."

Many mothers and their giggling daughters hurried out with brooms. The courtyard rang with laughter as they worked. María laughed louder than anyone. She pushed her stiff sagebrush broom as fast as she could. She made it into a game to see who finished first.

Sharing her duties in the courtyard and in the house made time go quickly for María. She spent hours playing

string games with her sisters and making little pots in the playhouse. She was so busy she almost forgot about the pilgrimage and how important she was.

Then long before the sun was up one morning, Mother awakened María. "Get up," she whispered. "Father is waiting. You are making your pilgrimage today."

María rubbed her eyes and smiled at Mother. "May I wear my new dress?" she whispered. "And my new boots?"

"Aie," Mother replied.

After a light breakfast María waved to Mother. She and Father started down the road past Black Mesa. Once, she turned back to see Desidéria and Ana glaring at her. They were angry.

María knew they wanted to walk to Chimayo but they had to stay home. It was her pilgrimage and only she would go with Father. Mother and Uncle would ride in the wagon. María giggled. She really was special.

For the first few miles María skipped behind Father, watching for birds and chipmunks. Soon she became tired and needed to rest. Before she could ask Father to stop she heard his deep, melodic voice. It sounded like the beat of the drum at sacred dances. He was praying.

María listened for a moment, then slipped up behind him. Softly she joined in the chant with him: "Our Father Who art in heaven . . ." After saying the entire prayer five times, they prayed the Hail Mary. They recited it five times, too.

María clasped her little holy medal tightly as she prayed. Mother warned her not to lose it. She said María would need it at the Santuario, the church, in Chimayo.

As they prayed, the soft winds rustled in the trees and the birds chirped loudly. When they finished praying, María checked her white moccasin boots. They were new and she did not want to soil them. She ran her fingers down the front of her new dress. It was purple . . . her favorite color.

After they walked for a long time, María noticed Father looking at the sun. He could tell time by its position in the sky. María knew it was time for lunch since the shadows had slipped under the rocks to hide.

"You need to eat, María," Father said, handing her three tortillas and a small jar of water.

María chose a cool, shady place under an old cottonwood tree to eat. She laughed when piñon jays scolded them and frightened chipmunks darted nervously about. They peeked at her from behind the scrub cedar bushes. María was hungry but she broke off small portions of the tortillas and tossed them to the jays and chipmunks.

When she finished eating she wiped her mouth and hands with a small cloth she carried in her pocket. She noticed that Father had not eaten. He was staring into the distance. It was impolite to watch another eat.

"Where's your lunch?"

"Adults don't eat on a pilgrimage," he said. "Only children are allowed to eat, especially you, since you are still weak." María didn't know adults didn't eat on a pilgrimage. She was glad she was a child. She had been hungry and enjoyed her food.

"We'd better get going," Father said, glancing at the sky. They had lost a lot of time while María ate. "We still have halfway to go."

"I can make it," María replied, wiping the dust from her boots. "The food helped. . . . I'm not tired anymore."

The sun was low in the sky when María and Father trudged into Chimayo. It had been a long walk. María's legs ached and she was thirsty. Her water bottle was empty.

María saw Mother and Uncle waiting in the wagon near the Santuario. *I won't have to walk back to the pueblo,* she thought. *I can ride in the wagon.* She wanted to run to the wagon. She wanted to crawl in it and rest. She was tired and needed a nap.

"Come on," Mother said, pulling María away from the wagon. "We must hurry. It's getting late. You must thank Santo Niño." Holding Mother's hand, María walked obediently into the church. Father and Uncle waited in the wagon.

Walking into the church María forgot she was tired. She was eager to see the saint who saved her life. *He must be beautiful,* she thought, imagining a clean, well-dressed saint, with big, brown eyes and curly hair.

Inside the church she wrinkled her nose. *I wonder if this damp-smelling place really is the Santuario of Santo Niño.* She shivered. She was disappointed. She expected something bright and cheerful like her church at the pueblo.

"Why would he choose such a cold place?" she murmured, moving softly over the hard dirt floor.

María wrinkled her nose again. With a tinge of shame she quickly made the sign of the cross. She didn't want to offend him. Humbly, she made her way to a row of fluttering votive candles. *Maybe I should light one,* she thought, watching the yellow candles flicker.

Just then a painted figure on the altar caught her eye. It was Santo Niño. María was shocked. His shoes were dirty and worn. She had been told that he walked many miles to help sick children. But she didn't think his shoes would be in such bad shape. A saint deserved something better.

"I walked ten miles today," María said, looking up at him. "A mile for each of my years." Again, she looked at his dirty shoes and then down at her own clean boots. She had wiped her boots each time she found dust on them.

She ran her fingers over the floral pattern in her purple dress. It was not soiled from the long dusty walk. She loved her dress. It made her feel special.

"I am special," she whispered to Santo Niño. "Was it not I who made the pilgrimage to see you? Not Desidéria. Nor

Ana." María remembered how sad her sisters looked when she told them goodbye. She remembered how angry they were, too.

"Only I was allowed to go," she said, tossing her head. Just thinking about it made her feel proud. "It's wrong to be proud," she giggled. "But I don't care." Quickly she pressed her hand against her mouth. She looked at Santo Niño to see if he was enjoying her humor. The look on his face disturbed her. Was he displeased? She couldn't tell.

She turned to see if Mother had heard. She hadn't. Mother was kneeling beside a grilled gate. Her bright red shawl was pulled low over her face as she prayed. María stared as Mother's fingers moved over the rosary.

María turned back to Santo Niño. She liked him . . . even if his shoes were dirty and worn. She wanted to make him talk to her. She leaned closer to him. But he didn't say a word.

Just then a sharp clang of the gate startled her. Whirling around she saw the caretaker, an old man, unlocking the gate. When he finished he took the key out of the lock and hung it on his belt. María watched him shuffle slowly out the side door. After he left she realized he had unlocked the gate for her.

Frightened, she edged closer to Santo Niño. He never acknowledged her presence. He never blinked an eye. Helplessly, she looked at the votive candles flickering like patches of bright flowers.

Slowly she moved over to the gate. She sensed a deep recess beyond it. She had to go through it. It was scary. Finally she placed her hands on the grilled design and peered through. She saw nothing, nothing but darkness.

María stiffened. *If this is where I have to go to thank Santo Niño,* she thought, trembling, *I won't do it. I will tell him so.*

Going back to the altar, she edged closer to Santo Niño. She wanted to get as far away as possible from that gate.

"Please help me," she begged, looking up at him. "Please." There was no response.

She turned toward the comforting glow of the votive candles. She should have lighted one when she came in. It might have helped. Maybe it wasn't too late.

"María," Mother called softly. "Come over here. You must go to the room below." María didn't move. Her feet felt as wooden as Santo Niño's. "Hurry, María."

"It's . . . dark . . . down . . . there," she whispered.

"There's nothing to be afraid of," Mother urged. "But be careful. The steps are steep. Count them as you go."

María knew she had to go down to the room, dark or not. Mother had made a promise. A promise must be kept.

"I'll go down there," she murmured, straightening her shoulders. "I'll never run from fear. Never!"

CHAPTER FOUR

The Healing

Standing straight as one of Grandfather's arrows, María peered down into the darkness. She shivered. Then probing with the tip of her moccasin she found the first step. She reached for the second one as she held her breath. Touching it, she moved slowly, ever so slowly, searching for the next step and the next.

"I wonder why it's so dark and cold in here?" she murmured. "It smells, too. Like a damp storehouse for corn and squash." Yet it wasn't quite the same.

She twitched her nose. No. It didn't smell like that. Nor did it smell like where they stored pots, especially at Tía Nicolasa's. But Old Grandmother's storehouse was different. It was a place of dry warmth and dust—even mystery . . . almost spooky.

María rubbed her nose. She wished she were there now. Mother had promised that they would go through the storehouse someday soon. They had to wait for Old Grandmother to tell them when to open it. Spooky or not it would be fun.

Trembling, she probed for the next step. She was almost there. She wondered why the steps were so far apart and so steep. They must have been made for people with long legs.

When she reached the bottom she made the sign of the cross. Making a pilgrimage wasn't fun. It was scary. For a moment she longed for Desidéria and Ana.

I'd better hurry, she thought, clutching her holy medal. It was the only tool she had to dig the sacred soil from the walls of the room. Where should she start? She couldn't see anything—nothing—not a cross, a votive candle, or even Santo Niño. It was too dark. *Something's wrong,* she whimpered. *I can't see!*

"I'm blind!" she cried. "The spotted sickness left me blind." She wondered if Santo Niño had punished her for being proud. Being proud was wrong. "I'll never see the apple blossoms again . . .," she said softly. "Or . . . the . . . little . . . yellow . . . pond . . . lily."

"María."

Startled, María turned toward Mother's voice and looked up. Mother was sitting just inside the gate. María blinked. She saw Mother. She wasn't blind! Perhaps her eyes hadn't adjusted to the darkness.

"María," Mother said, "say your prayers. Say them loud enough so I can hear them."

"Our Father Who art in heaven," María chanted, beginning to undress. Mother had told her to remove her clothing as soon as she reached the bottom. But she had forgotten. Carefully she placed her new dress on top of her boots.

"Hallowed . . . be . . . Thy . . ." Her voice faltered. *I wonder how long this will take?* she thought, then remembering her prayers almost shouted, "Name!"

When she finished her prayers, María moved her fingers gently over the ridges in the wall where pilgrims before her had scraped the sacred soil. Eagerly, she worked until she had a small handful of dirt. "Thank you, Santo Niño," she prayed, rubbing the dirt over her body. "Thank you for making me well."

The more dirt she rubbed on her body the better she felt. It warmed her. It felt good in her hands. It had the same feeling as the dirt from the acequia, the kind she made into pots.

Why, this is Mother Earth! She covered her mouth to stifle a surprised giggle. She had believed Mother Earth was just on her pueblo.

When she finished rubbing her body she started to dress. *This isn't bad, even if it soils my dress,* she thought, holding a handful of the sacred soil. *It makes me feel good.*

Humming quietly she filled the small water jar with the dirt. She had carried the jar in her pocket all the way to the Santuario. Quickly she climbed the steps. They didn't seem so strange now. Maybe her legs had grown some. Seconds later she appeared at the top of the steps. She looked at the votive candles and smiled. *They look different now,* she thought. *Almost as pretty as the flowers on my purple dress.*

Mother handed María a small bundle. It was her offering to Santo Niño. María walked over to the altar and smiled at the saint.

Your shoes aren't so bad, she thought, unfolding the bundle. Still smiling at him, she placed a large piece of buckskin on the altar. *Perhaps this will make you a new pair of shoes.* Next she rubbed her fingers over a small black rosary and placed it beside the buckskin. Carefully, she placed three ten-cent pieces near the rosary.

María kept her eyes on the coins. They seemed to carry a message for her. But like Santo Niño they spoke no words. She looked at Santo Niño and smiled. She hoped he liked his gifts.

When she and Mother left the Santuario, María never looked back. They met Father and Uncle standing near the wagon. Uncle lifted María into the wagon. Then Father, Mother, and Uncle crowded together in the seat. Uncle flipped the horses' reins and the wagon rolled down the road.

As the wagon bounced over the rough road, María stretched out her short legs. Her white boots were still clean. They reminded her of Santo Niño's dirty shoes. She started to giggle but placed her hand over her mouth. That would not have been polite. Instead, she wriggled her toes and watched the soft buckskin move up and down over her foot.

"What will I do with this?" she asked, handing Mother the small jar of dirt.

"You will mix it with water and drink it," Mother replied. "You will drink some every day for four days. It will keep you well."

"Do all the pilgrims drink the sacred dirt with water?" María asked. She wasn't too sure she wanted to. She liked the feel of it on her body but she didn't think it would taste very good. Mother nodded.

María tucked her head down inside her shawl. *If I drink this mixture,* she thought, *I will feel good on the inside just like I did on the outside. Maybe I will feel good the rest of my life.*

CHAPTER FIVE

Summertime

María soon forgot about the pilgrimage and how important she was. She kept busy making little pots in the playhouse. One morning Mother asked her to help pack some dishes. "We are going to Jacona for the summer," she said. "We will need to take our cooking pots."

"I don't want to go," María said, looking out the window at the plaza. Who would sweep it if she was at Jacona? She loved the plaza with the big cottonwood tree standing in the middle. The tree was much older than María. She liked to run her fingers over its thick bark and she liked to sit in its shade.

This is my home, María thought. *I don't want to leave it. Never!*

"Let me stay with Tía Nicolasa," she begged as Mother packed another pot in a big basket.

"No, María," Mother murmured. "Families must stay together. You will go with us."

When it was time to go María obediently climbed up on the heavy wagon and nestled down beside Desidéria and Ana. Father made a clicking sound with his tongue and flicked the reins and María felt the wagon jolt down the road. Ana and Desidéria waved to friends watching them leave, but María never looked back.

She pulled her blanket up around her neck and lay back on her pillows. Sadly she watched fleecy, white clouds as they floated across the sky. Shutting out her sisters' chatter, she listened to a distant rumble of thunder and noticed dark thunderheads moving slowly toward them. She expected rain any moment. María saw Father look at the sky. He cracked the whip and urged the horses to go faster.

A few hours later the wagon turned off onto a rocky road and bounced down along a river. Startled, María peered at the strange road and murky water. The river was the same muddy color as the acequia at home. Thinking about the ditch reminded her of their playhouse. *I wish I were there now,* she thought. *I'd be making pots.* She worked her fingers as if making a pot. She could almost feel the clay in her hands.

The wagon moved slowly along the river. María wondered if they would ever get to Jacona. It was such a long trip. *At least the thunderclouds are drifting away,* she thought. They were taking away the threat of rain.

This seems like a long road going somewhere, she thought. *But it's not in a hurry to get there. I'm not in a hurry to get there either.*

When they finally arrived at their summer home María noticed the look on Mother's face. She felt Mother was disappointed with their new home. It wasn't what she expected. Somehow the house wasn't what Father had described but like Mother she just smiled when she saw it.

María listened as Mother talked to Father. "It's beautiful," she said, looking at their new home. "Just what I wanted."

Inside, she whispered to the girls. "Help me put things in order. Everything is backwards from what I need. We'll leave it this way for a few days. When we change it he won't notice."

The summer at Jacona seemed long and hot to María although she didn't complain. She kept busy carrying cool water to Ana and Father as they worked in the fields. She helped Mother in the house, too, but never once stopped thinking about her home at the pueblo.

In her mind she was always at the playhouse on the acequia making little pots. Time and again she worked an imaginary ball of clay between her little fingers. She imagined the pots as beautiful as the ones Old Grandmother and Tía Nicolasa made.

Desidéria suggested they play string games but María shook her head. She was tired of string games. She already knew how to make the rope corral, stars, and turkey claws. She could even make the harder ones like two women walking toward each other and the shooting arrow. She preferred making new pictures of her own.

When summer was almost over Father and Ana began to harvest the crops. María had never seen so many pumpkins, baskets of squash, and ears of corn. Father had raised enough food to help others. No one would go hungry during the long winter months. That made María happy. That was worth being away from home all summer.

One day they loaded up the wagon and started home. María sat facing the front of the wagon, watching for familiar places. She smiled when she saw the old tree where she had eaten lunch on her pilgrimage. It seemed so long ago to her now.

The tree looked different. Suddenly she realized that everything looked different—almost backwards. *It's like flipping the pages of a book from the back and trying to read it.* She giggled.

As the wagon bounced over the deep ruts, María planned what she would do when she got home. First she would go see Tía Nicolasa and Old Grandmother. Then she would make pots.

As they neared the pueblo María faced forward once

more. She saw the old cottonwood tree on the plaza. It stood tall and stately like a sentinel watching over them. María believed that the tree did guard the pueblo. *I feel safe . . . and blessed,* she thought, making the sign of the cross. *Almost as if I were in church.*

After everything was put in the storehouse, María ran to visit Tía Nicolasa. Desidéria tagged along behind. "Why are you going there?" Desidéria pouted. "I want to play pretend mothers."

"Then you play," retorted María. "I'm going to learn to make pots. Good pots."

Tía Nicolasa was surprised to see the girls. "Hello and welcome," she said, opening the door wide. "Come in, come in. What can I do for you? Did Mother send you for something?"

"No," Desidéria said irritably, looking at María.

"Teach me to make pots," María said, looking down at her feet. It was rude to look anyone in the face. "You know." She hesitated. "The kind you . . . and . . . Old Grandmother make."

"All right. We'll make pots," Tía Nicolasa replied with a smile. "But first we must eat lunch."

María wasn't hungry. She thought they would never finish eating. It seemed to take almost as long as when they went to Jacona.

After they cleaned the kitchen they went to a shady place on the north side of the house. María watched silently as her aunt put all the materials together. María fidgeted but didn't speak. She had a million questions she wanted to ask Tía Nicolasa.

She wanted to get started. She wanted to make a pot. *Maybe I should help her,* she thought. *But no,* she remembered. *The Indian way is to watch.*

CHAPTER SIX

New Beginnings

"You shouldn't pester your aunt," Mother scolded. "She has too much work for you to bother her."

"I think Tía Nicolasa enjoyed helping me," María said, hanging her head, but promised not to bother her aunt again.

The next morning María slipped out the door. She hurried to the north side of the house, hoping Desidéria wouldn't know where she was. María wanted to be alone. She knew that Desidéria would want to play pretend mothers and string games but she wanted to make pots.

María went over all the things she had watched Tía Nicolasa do. Soon she had all the clay, water, and sand assembled. María had never used sand before. Tía Nicolasa said it made the pots stronger and held them together.

Taking a pinch of sacred cornmeal from her apron pocket, María tossed it into the four directions: first to the north, the south, the east, and then the west. At the same time she prayed to Mother Earth. María asked her to guide her so she wouldn't do inferior work. She didn't want to dishonor Mother Earth.

Kneeling in the shade of the house María worked slowly. Tía Nicolasa warned her not to work too fast or it might ruin the pot. A small breeze brushed against her cheek. She loved the wind but she loved the little lump of clay in her hand better. It seemed to be a part of her, just as it was a part of the whole pueblo. That included all the people, the trees, and even the earth she kneeled upon.

María looked at the clay. She squeezed it. It was almost the same color as her hand. For a moment she studied it. Did it speak to her? She thought so. Maybe it had a message for her. María didn't know. Just like Santo Niño, it didn't say a word.

María longed to tell the clay how she wanted to make pots. She didn't want to work in the fields like Ana. She didn't want to go to school either, especially not a school away from home, as far away as Santa Fe.

"I can't talk to you," she whispered, "but I can make you into a beautiful pot."

Carefully, ever so carefully, she pressed part of the clay flat onto her palm. It looked like a pancake with a deep hand print on it. Pleased, she placed it on a small plate.

She broke off small pieces of clay and rolled them into long sausage-shaped rolls. Piece by piece she built a wall around the edge of the clay disk. Using her fingertips as tools, she sealed the pieces together. When she was done, María gasped. It wasn't a pot. It was a strange, lopsided brown glob with a hole in it.

What happened to it? María wondered, clasping her hands together. *It doesn't look like Tía Nicolasa's or Old Grandmother's pots. It looks more like a mud pie.*

Stunned, María didn't move. She didn't know what to do. She used sand like Tía Nicolasa said to make it stronger. What would Mother Earth think? Had María dishonored her?

She sadly rolled the pot into a ball. Tía Nicolasa couldn't fire it now. No one could, not even Old Grandmother.

I can't give up, she thought. *I'll try again tomorrow. And all the other tomorrows. However long it takes. I will make pots. Great pots!*

Tía Nicolasa laughed when María told her about the lopsided pot. María hung her head. She was afraid Tía Nicolasa would think she had not listened well.

"Aie, aie, aie, María," she said, placing her arms around her niece. "It's the same with all potters. We all have accidents. We are lucky when we lose only one or two in a firing."

"Do you have accidents?"

"Of course, child," Tía Nicolasa said.

"But not Old Grandmother?"

"Yes, Old Grandmother, too," Tía Nicolasa said, smoothing her apron. "Did you know that Old Grandmother has quit making pots? She says she's tired."

"That's all right," María said. "Old Grandmother has a storehouse full of pots. She doesn't need to work anymore."

"Aie," Tía Nicolasa replied, nodding. "We won't be making pots much longer either. Winter will soon be here. We don't make pots when it's cold."

María shivered and looked at the skies. "It's cold now. But I'll make them."

"No, you will be going to school."

"I don't want to go to school," María said. "Do you think I have to?"

Tía Nicolasa nodded.

"I need to talk to Mother about school," María said. "I'll see you later." She hurried out the door.

A few weeks later María started school. She begged to stay at home but Mother said no. María was afraid to go to school because she spoke Tewa, her native tongue, and Spanish. Her teacher spoke English.

However, María was smart and in a short time she learned English, too. She liked her teacher and they became good friends. Later, when her parents visited school, María proudly interpreted what Miss Grimes said to them.

At the end of the school year María decided she wanted

to learn even more. She asked Miss Grimes to give her extra lessons. So they worked together when María had time. María swept the floors, washed windows, and carried in wood to pay for the lessons.

María was an excellent student. Miss Grimes recommended that she go to an advanced school. Her parents talked it over with the governor of the pueblo. They agreed to send her to St. Catherine's, a boarding school, in Santa Fe. It was decided that Desidéria would go along and they could stay there for two years. María's parents wanted her to become a teacher and teach at the pueblo.

At first María didn't like St. Catherine's. It was harder for her than the school at the pueblo. She didn't like the nuns either. They were too strict and they never laughed.

María liked Sister Brigita, her sewing teacher. She didn't mind if the girls talked and laughed. But they had to do it quietly. María discovered that she liked sewing. She was good at it.

Sister Brigita noticed how well María worked with her hands and praised her one day. María was pleased and all day had a grand feeling about herself. When she heard Father Antonio talk about the sin of pride she became sad. He said it was one of the seven deadly sins sent by the devil.

María was so ashamed that she went to bed that night and thought about all the things she didn't do well—especially writing. She had coaxed Desidéria into writing her weekly letters to their parents. Later she copied them. In exchange María darned Desidéria's stockings.

At the end of two years Mother Superior presented María with a picture of Saint Joseph. She said María was the best seamstress the school had had for a long time. Desidéria was awarded a little figure of the Sacred Heart for her proficiency in English.

María went to see Miss Grimes when she returned to the pueblo. Miss Grimes was proud of María. She encouraged her to get more education. "I agree with your parents," she said. "I think you should become a teacher."

"I don't want to," María murmured. "I would have to leave the pueblo to learn more. I won't ever leave again."

"María, it's a big world out there. There are many things to see," coaxed Miss Grimes. "You could visit the Statue of Liberty, the Battery, and Fifth Avenue in New York." María shook her head. "You could always come back to the pueblo. You could teach here . . . maybe take my place."

Again, María shook her head. "I just want to work for you. And make pots." Satisfied that she had convinced her teacher that she wouldn't leave the pueblo, María started working for her.

After cleaning the school every day, she made pots. Some were big and some were small. Some cracked and others broke. She never became discouraged. With each one she improved her skill and worked harder.

María helped Mother sell her cheese, too. She was very successful at it. Mother thought she was a good trader with the bargains she made. Sometimes she got money or ground cornmeal, and once two silver buttons.

"You are a good trader, María," Mother said. "Much better than I."

"I like to trade," María answered. "When I grow up I'm going to have a trading post all my own. I will sell all kinds of things. Even pots."

Although María liked making pots, she liked working for her teacher, too. She wanted to please Miss Grimes. One day as she completed her chores she noticed the woodbox was low. There wasn't much wood outside either. She would have to chop some.

"María," Miss Grimes said the next day. "We are going to need some more wood if we are to keep warm. I don't think you can split it into smaller pieces."

"I can try, Miss Grimes."

"No, you can't," she said. "Neither can I. Why don't you ask your father if he knows anyone who can help us?"

That night María asked Father if he knew someone

who would work for Miss Grimes. Father thought for a moment, then nodded. "Julián Martínez might," he said. "He helps his father make sifters and saddles. They aren't much for farming though. Especially Julián."

"I'll tell her," María answered, continuing to read the book Miss Grimes lent her. She hoped Miss Grimes would like Julián and he would be a good worker but she doubted it. *Julián was a bad boy,* she thought. He ran away from school and wouldn't do his lessons. If he wasn't much of a farmer maybe he couldn't chop wood either. But she'd tell Miss Grimes just the same.

Arriving at the school the next day María found the door standing open. Miss Grimes wasn't there but María thought she'd return soon. She noticed that the blackboard was full of writing. She would have to clean it. She knew it was better to start the day with a clean, fresh board. That way the children wouldn't be confused with yesterday's lessons. Just as she started cleaning the blackboard she heard someone at the door. Thinking it was Miss Grimes she said, "This is hard work but I'll get it all off before the day starts."

"That's good," a deep voice said in Tewa.

Startled, María turned and at first she didn't recognize the tall lean man standing there. Glancing at his face she knew it was Julián. "Did you come to chop wood?" she blurted out before she thought. To ask a direct question was impolite so she hung her head and stared at the floor.

"Yes," Julián said, looking down at the floor, too. "I came to chop wood." He didn't move for so long that María wondered if he had lost something on the floor or if he thought she needed to sweep it again. "I'll go find Miss Grimes," he finally said, and María heard his soft moccasins move swiftly across the floor.

Suddenly it seemed important to María to scrub the blackboard until it shone. She rubbed so hard that her fingers became numb. When she was sure Julián was gone she picked up her shawl and started home.

The next day Julián came to chop wood. He came the next day and the next. María listened for the sound of the axe as it hit the wood. The steady "chop-chop-chop" made her heart thump. She had to place her hand over her heart to try to calm it as she thought of Julián. She hadn't remembered how handsome he was.

In spite of the excitement he created in her, María did notice that the woodpile was getting higher and higher. *He may not be much of a farmer,* she thought. *But he sure can cut wood.*

"I don't think we'll be cold for a long time," Miss Grimes laughed. "I'll tell Julián we don't need any more wood."

The next day, when María saw Julián with his axe, she giggled as her hand flew over her mouth. "Why are you here?" she asked, then realized she had spoken too soon. "Miss Grimes said we didn't need any more wood."

Julián smiled shyly. "I don't speak English," he said, with a twinkle in his eye. "I didn't know what she said." He put his axe away and helped María sweep the floor. Afterwards he walked her up the hill and home.

The next day he was there to help her sweep the floor and to walk her home again. María wanted to laugh. She had been running up and down that hill all her life and no one had ever accompanied her—not until now.

If Miss Grimes noticed that María and Julián were spending a lot of time together she didn't say anything, not to María nor to anyone else. "I don't think you will become a teacher, María," she muttered to herself after watching Julián walk María home.

CHAPTER SEVEN

The Prophecy

Mother was a different story. She watched everything María did. She knew exactly how much time they spent together.

"You see a lot of Julián," she said. María nodded. She hadn't thought about it, but she saw him most every day.

"Does it mean something to you?" Mother asked. María didn't answer. She just hung her head.

"Do you think you mean anything to him?" Mother persisted.

María kept her head down. "I think so," she murmured.

"When a couple sees that much of one another people begin to talk. They expect you to marry."

"It's none of their business," María retorted angrily.

"You are wrong, María. Anything that happens in the pueblo is a little bit everyone's business."

"No!" María protested. "It's my business."

"Do you want to marry Julián?"

"I hadn't thought about it," María admitted.

"If you choose to marry you should pick a good man. A man that will farm and take care of you."

"Julián is good even if he doesn't farm!" María turned to look at the old cottonwood tree. She felt that it gave her courage, and strength.

"He isn't bad, but Felipe's parents have already been here to talk about you," Mother said. "Felipe wants to marry you."

"I won't marry Felipe!" María's eyes flashed. "Never!"

"Think about it, María," Mother said softly. "Felipe already has his own land and he is a good farmer."

"No, I don't want to marry anyone," María replied, wrapping her shawl around her shoulders. "I'm going to see Tía Nicolasa. She fired this morning and I want to see how my pot turned out."

María found Tía Nicolasa sorting out the pots. There was a big smile on her face. "Look, María," she cried. "Your water jar came out perfect. It didn't even crack but my little one did."

"Mine . . . perfect?"

"Yes, this one." She held up the pot María had made a few days before. "You are going to be a fine potter, María. This is a real jar." She smiled as María inspected it. "You will always have good luck with your pots because your first piece turned out all right."

"May I give this to Mother?"

"I think she would like that," Tía Nicolasa said, handing the pot to María. "You know, making pots isn't a game."

"I know, Tía," María whispered. "I love making pots. It's all I want to do."

"You may forget about it for awhile. With school, cold weather . . . and other things." She raised her head and studied María.

"Nothing can make me forget about pots," María said. "Nothing."

"When summer comes and you try again you will make a fine potter."

"I will go back to it," María promised. "And now, I want to give this jar to Mother."

Mother praised and admired the jar, then set it in the

nicho above the fireplace where everyone could see it. *I'm glad Mother likes the jar,* María thought. *Now maybe she will forget about Felipe.*

One morning María heard voices in the kitchen. She peeked around the door to see who was visiting at that time of day. It was Uncle. She wanted to rush in and greet him but she stood back. That would be impolite. Besides, his voice sounded serious as he talked to Mother, so she went to the other room and waited.

After Uncle left, Mother grabbed her shawl and called to María. "Hurry," she said. "Old Grandmother has sent for us. She wants all her family there. Even the children."

"Why?"

"Because she feels well today," Mother said. "She thinks she may never feel that well again."

María couldn't picture Old Grandmother feeling well. The last time she saw her she looked bad. She was all shrunk into herself. She looked like a tiny little girl lying on her bed.

Even her voice had shrunk. It was faint and twittering like a bird. When María put her head close to Old Grandmother's mouth she couldn't hear what she said.

"What does she want?" María asked.

"You'll see," Mother replied.

When they arrived at Old Grandmother's she was lying on her bed on the floor. Her small beady eyes were staring at her family gathered around her. Usually, she was watching the fire in the fireplace or looking out the window at Black Mesa.

Suddenly Old Grandmother started speaking. Her voice was stronger and bigger than María had ever heard it. She leaned forward to listen. She didn't want to miss a word. *Old Grandmother must have saved her voice,* she thought. *She doesn't have to whisper now.*

"I'll be going away soon," Old Grandmother said. "It happens to all old people." She stopped to rest her voice and after several moments spoke again.

"Give my dance costumes and jewelry to my grand-daughters." She rested her voice again as her family waited.

What a wise woman, María thought. *She saved her voice as she did other things . . . especially pots.*

"Divide my pots among my granddaughters," she said, gasping for air. "My daughter gets my house." Old Grand-mother closed her eyes and gasped. "That is all I have to say. Go home now."

"Mother, is Old Grandmother going to die?" María asked, as they started up the hill toward their house.

"We don't know."

"Old Grandmother thinks so," María said. "If she doesn't know, why does she talk like that?"

"Old people do that sometimes," Mother said, trying to comfort her. "But they don't really know."

A few days later when Grandmother started to feed Old Grandmother some atole she noticed that her mother wasn't breathing. Old Grandmother had gone away, as she told them she would.

When the funeral and customary feasting were over, the daughters gathered to open Old Grandmother's store-house. It was built off Old Grandmother's kitchen. It hadn't been used for years. When they finally pried the door open, a smell like no other rushed out to meet them. It was a special kind of odor . . . like musty dried squash, seed corn, cured meat, and even adobe.

"María, you and Desidéria may remove the pots," Mother said. "It will be easy for you girls. You are smaller than the rest of us."

María felt excited and important as she stepped over the doorstone to the storeroom. Quickly she looked around the room. She gasped and her hand flew over her mouth.

She had never seen so many pots. They were beautiful! There were red ones, white ones, and others with designs on them. Some of the designs were pressed on and some had been painted in fine delicate strokes. The bear claw seemed to be a favorite design.

In the corner a huge red pot caught María's eye. She ran her finger over the pot, leaving a clean streak where she wiped off the dust. Then she carried it out of the room.

Carefully, she continued to move out the bigger pots, leaving the small ones for Desidéria. But her mind never left the big red pot. When they divided up the pots they gave María the red one. Mother had noticed how much she liked it.

I will fill this full of popcorn and put it in our storehouse for winter, she thought. *When we have storytelling nights we can eat it then.* She held the pot tenderly in her arms as she carried it home. She had never seen one like it—so well shaped, so thin. It was beautiful! It wasn't thick and crude like some pots she had seen in the pueblo. "Someday, Old Grandmother," she whispered, stroking the pot, "I will make one as perfect as this. I will be a potter like you."

CHAPTER EIGHT

The Proposal

After that María was on the shady side of the house early every morning making pots. All her thoughts were of making pots as fine as Old Grandmother's. She worked hard to perfect her skill. She was determined to make the best pots ever. *I hope someone will like my pots enough to fill them with popcorn,* she thought one day as her hands smoothed the rough places on a piece she was working on. She was so engrossed in her work that she never heard the soft moccasin steps approaching her.

A long shadow fell across the yard just as she finished her pot. Glancing up, she saw Julián. *I wonder what he wants this time of day?* she thought. *It must be important.* Usually she saw him at night after the chores were all finished.

Shyly she dropped her head and quickly put her hand inside the pot. She pressed her palm against the side to make a deep imprint. *I hope Julián notices this pot,* she thought. *It is the biggest one I've ever made. Just like Old Grandmother's.*

Julián stood silently watching María but she never raised her eyes. "Are you going to decorate that pot?" he finally asked.

"No," María said. "I don't know how."

"I know how," he declared. María laughed. He would probably decorate it the same way he farmed—not very well.

"My uncle came to see me," Julián said, changing the subject. María nodded and waited. What did his uncle have to do with decorating her pot?

"Uncle said the Indian Agency wants some Indians to go to St. Louis."

"Why?"

"They're having a World's Fair there," he said, looking at her. "Nineteen-oh-four, a big year for St. Louis! They want the Indians to dance and sing."

"How long will they stay?" she asked, wiping her hands on an old cloth.

"A long time. Maybe four or five months." He began slapping his hand nervously against his leg as if beating a drum. "Maybe even longer." For a while he was silent. Then he said, "They have a place for them to live. And they will pay for traveling."

"Is that all?" she asked.

"No," he said. "They will pay for singing and dancing, too."

María sat silently staring at her pot. It was almost perfect . . . not as thin as Old Grandmother's but nice.

"Do you want to go?" Julián asked.

María looked at her muddy hands lying in her lap. Finally she raised her head and stared at him. "Felipe Gonzales's parents came to see mine," she murmured. There was another silence.

"Are you going to marry him?" Julián asked, returning her stare.

"I don't know yet."

"What are you waiting for?" he asked, grinning. "Me?"

"I . . . guess . . . so . . . ," she said. "Yes."

"Well, I'd better go home and send my parents to visit yours," he said. "I won't let you marry Felipe."

After Julián left, María smiled and cleaned up her mess. *Julián wants to marry me!* She set the big pot near the house to dry. *It's my best pot yet. Maybe Tía Nicolasa will fire it.* In the back of her mind she wondered what Julián meant when he said he could decorate it. *Could* he really decorate it? And how?

After the evening meal was over and the dishes were washed, María waited for a knock on the door. It was getting late and no knock came. She was so nervous she clasped and unclasped her hands. Maybe Julián changed his mind. Maybe he didn't want to marry her.

María's head began to ache. She felt ashamed. She was glad no one else knew of her shame. All she wanted to do was go to bed and cover up her head. "Why did he say he would send his parents?" she cried silently, as the shame grew as big as her pot.

Suddenly there was a knock on the door. "It must be the neighbors," Father said, going to answer it. Mother looked at María.

"You should go to your room," she said. "Hurry now."

As the door opened, María closed her eyes. What if it were Felipe's parents? What would she say? She wouldn't marry Felipe, not even if Julián didn't want her. María's heart pounded. She was still afraid to look.

"Welcome," she heard Father say, and she opened her eyes. Julián's parents were standing there.

María's heart pounded loudly. She wanted to dance and sing. Instead she hurried from the room as if a grizzly bear were after her.

María's parents were afraid that Julián wouldn't provide for her as his wife. Anyone who didn't farm wasn't much of a man in their opinion. But they made preparations for the wedding anyway. It was what María wanted.

"You will have to stay married, María, even if it is bad," Mother said. "It is against the rules of the church and the pueblo to get a divorce."

María assured her that she would be a good wife and that everything would work out fine. "Julián will be a good husband, too," she said.

The next few weeks were busy ones. There was a lot of work to be done. All the aunts and most of the cousins came to help clean the house and paint the rooms. It was the custom.

While some of them painted and cleaned, others prepared tasty food. All the while laughter rang throughout the house as they joked and teased one another.

María was busy—very busy. She had to grind a basketful of cornmeal for Julián's mother. She was determined to show her future mother-in-law that she was not lazy and would make a good wife.

She sat on the floor and pushed the ears of corn over the rough stone. The harder she worked the less satisfied she was with the cornmeal. She let a small portion sift through her fingers and it was still too coarse. It had to be as fine as flour. She tried again and wanted to quit.

At last, when it was fine enough, she found an old apron in the kitchen and sifted the cornmeal through it. "That's all I can do," she murmured, placing it in a basket, then stepping out the door to go see Julián's mother.

"What have you here?" Mrs. Martínez asked, although she already knew. She raised the cover and looked at the cornmeal. After studying it for a long time she smiled at María. "I think that you will be a good wife for my son," she said. María knew that she was pleased.

Eighty people crowded into the house the day of the wedding. There were aunts, uncles, cousins, friends, babies, and children of all ages. María smiled at Julián as they waited for the ceremony to begin. Her wedding clothes were presents from Julián's parents. María thought they were beautiful. She rubbed her hand over her blouse to feel its softness.

She wore two mantas made from the finest dark-blue

material. Underneath them was a flowered blouse with
blue silk sleeves and pink ruffles at the wrists. Her head
was covered with a pink scarf and an orange shawl
embroidered with many-colored flowers hung over her
shoulders. White-tanned deer-hide moccasins were draped
around her legs. The black soles were turned up around
her feet. María thought they were the finest moccasins she
had ever seen, even nicer than the ones she wore on her
pilgrimage.

Julián wore a blue and pink shirt that matched María's
blouse and had a striped blanket over his shoulders. His
long, dark hair was neatly braided and wrapped in red
handkerchiefs. His legs were covered with white buckskin
leggings with long fringes. The fringes barely touched his
beaded moccasins. The leggings belonged to his Uncle
Juan. Juan had lent them to him for the wedding.

María stole a shy glance at Julián. *He's so handsome,*
she thought. *He'll make a fine husband.*

Tía Nicolasa slipped up beside María. "I made this
especially for you," she whispered.

Tears welled up in María's eyes as she gazed at the gift.
It was the most beautiful wedding jar she had ever seen.
She wiped her eyes and ran her fingers over the cream-col-
ored background on the jar. She traced the red and black
water snakes and flowers with the tip of her finger as she
held the wedding jar close to her.

"The water snake is to bring you happiness," Tía Nicolasa said. "The flowers are for happiness, too."

María thanked her aunt. "It is beautiful," she murmured, but she never mentioned that someday she
planned to make a pot just as beautiful. That would be
boasting. Already she had made one almost as nice as Old
Grandmother's but Tía Nicolasa hadn't seen it yet.

After the traditional blessings from their parents, an
old man, a religious head of the pueblo, took the jar from
María. He dropped a pinch of medicine into the water and

gave it to María and Julián to drink. As they drank he prayed for them. When he finished praying he gave them a serious talk. María listened carefully to his words.

"Marriage is an important and sacred thing," he said. "You both should make an effort not to be foolish and hard on each other. You must make the people who love you proud that you are their children." Again he blessed them and then poured the remaining water from the jar on the ground. María smiled. *Julián is finally my husband,* she thought.

After the blessing the crowd began to dance and enjoy the feast. The table almost bent under the weight of the food. There were tamales, frijoles, stew, and atole. Cup after cup of milk and coffee were consumed. The coffee had lots of sugar in it and was a favorite of the young and old alike.

In the midst of dancing and singing a man knocked on the door. "I have come to take María and Julián to the train," he said. "It's getting late so they must hurry." María and Julián told everyone goodbye and climbed in the man's wagon. They had celebrated so long that they had to leave in their wedding clothes.

They were on their way to St. Louis to the World's Fair. They would show people what Indians looked like and how they lived. They would dance and sing for them, too.

Julián was excited and couldn't wait to get there and earn some money. But María didn't share his joy. *I don't want to dance and sing at the World's Fair,* she thought sadly as they drove away. *I don't want to leave the pueblo. Not now nor ever. Not even for money.*

CHAPTER NINE

The Fair

The train moved slowly across the country as it spewed soot and black smoke all over María and Julián's fine wedding clothes. María disliked what it did to their clothing but she disliked the train's loud, blaring horn even more. It hurt her ears each time it blasted at a herd of cattle standing on the railroad track or when they approached a small town.

Julián grinned at María's discomfort. But when a burly old gambler lighted up his stogie and made it hard to breathe, Julián didn't grin. Both he and María longed for fresh air and sunshine. They hadn't seen the sun since they left the pueblo. It rained every day they had been gone.

"We should have traveled in Father's wagon," María said, looking at their soiled clothing. This time Julián grinned. He was beginning to enjoy their wild adventure across the strange country. It was different from what they had at home.

"It's such a slow train," María complained. "It reminds me of when we went to Jacona. It was a long road going somewhere, but it wasn't in a hurry to get there. This train isn't in a hurry to get there either."

"Are you?"

"Aie!" she cried, covering her ears as the horn shrilled loudly. They looked out the window and saw a group of cattle running for their lives. One old bull stood his ground near the track and glared at them.

When they finally arrived at the fair the rain stopped. But the weather was hot and humid and María and Julián were constantly wiping their faces. They found it much worse than rain. María longed for their cool adobe home in New Mexico.

They settled down in the Indian Village that had been made for them and started making pots. It would be a little longer before they could begin dancing. They were weary from the long train ride.

Finally, when the sun went down and it cooled off a bit, Julián beat the tom-tom and María danced. Some of the people enjoyed their dances and clapped for them. Others made fun of them and said cruel things. María pretended not to understand them and kept dancing. Julián couldn't speak English and didn't know what they said. *I wish we were home,* María thought as she danced. *I dance better on our sacred ground, where the clay is cool to my feet.*

After a time people started buying pots. They asked endless questions and seemed genuinely interested in them. Before long María and Julián were selling more of their wares. They had to work hard all day to supply the demand. They had a small place near their living quarters where they fired their pots. María sat on the ground and made her pots as people watched.

After four months María wanted to go home. She was expecting a child and wanted it to be born at the pueblo. So they boarded a train and started back to San Ildefonso. "This train *is* going somewhere," she said, with a wide smile. "But it's not in a hurry to get there."

"Are you?" Julián teased.

"Aie!" she cried, looking at the flat land. "Aie!"

When they arrived at the pueblo they found a house

waiting for them. It was freshly painted and ready to move into. María's family had prepared it for them.

Not long after they arrived home some of their customers from the fair came to see them. They wanted more pots. They even brought friends with them to buy pots, too.

Friends told friends about them and soon they had more business than they could handle. Julián was trying to farm with María's father but he wasn't very good at it. So he built a small trading post onto their house and quit farming to sell pots and groceries. He knew more English now.

"You have your trading post," María's mother said to her one day. "Just like you told me you would." María remembered telling her mother that. It was something she had kept in mind.

María looked at the pots in the workshop. Most of them were already sold. Now they not only were making money but were becoming famous, too.

They had so much money that María decided to hide some of it. She had to find a safe place. She took down the picture of Saint Joseph and hammered a hole in the wall where he had hung. Quickly she put the money in the hole and covered it over with plaster. Soon Saint Joseph was hanging back where he belonged. No one ever knew that María had hidden the money—not even Julián.

During this time there was talk in the pueblo. People said that they were all supposed to be the same and yet Julián and María had more money than anyone. María remembered what her mother had said about her actions being a little bit of everyone's business.

"I think we should share our knowledge," María said, polishing a small pot. Julián nodded. He was busy making a design for María's pots. He wanted to surprise her. "I must help them," María continued. "God gave me the hands to make pots and Mother Earth gave me the luck."

Soon all the women were making pots and selling

them. When a woman couldn't sell her pots she took them to María and asked her to sell them for her. María picked out the best pot and signed her own name to it. When she sold the pot she gave the money to the woman.

One morning María found a pot in the workshop that had a design on it. For a moment she was puzzled, until she saw Julián watching her. "Did you do this?" she asked. Julián nodded, waiting to see if she liked it. "Then make some more," she said, looking at the design. "You are a better artist than a farmer."

By this time everything was going well for María and Julián. They now had a son, Adam, and were expecting another child. Business was good and María had enough money to help others. She enjoyed helping others and sharing her good fortune. She thanked Mother Earth for her good luck.

Early one morning, María's daughter came into the world. María's mother washed the baby in warm water and wrapped her in a clean square torn from the back of one of Julián's old shirts. She handed the baby to María.

María looked and looked at her baby daughter. "I have waited a long time for you," she whispered to the little one as she held her tiny finger. "And you are worth it."

"I am going to take your daughter up on the roof and introduce her to the world by her Indian name," Ana said, picking up the baby.

"And what is that?" María asked.

"The prettiest name I ever heard," she said, smiling at María. "Yellow Pond Lily."

When Julián came home at noon he wanted to see the baby. He couldn't see María. It was the Indian way for the husband to wait four days after a baby was born before seeing his wife.

Ana took the baby out of her swing-cradle beside María's bed and gave her to Julián. He threw back his head and laughed and laughed. He said the child should be named "Pottery-Colored Pond Lily" because she looked like a red pot that had just been fired. He didn't see anything yellow about her.

Eight days later Julián left for the Pajarito Plateau, where he went to work with an archaeologist to help with a dig. It would be several months before he could return. It was a long hard trip over the mountains and since there were no roads he would have to walk.

The day he left, María held the baby to Julián's face. He kissed first one of her cheeks, then the other. María felt tears form in her eyes when she noticed Julián crying. He held his daughter close and told her not to grow up too fast while he was away. "I'm afraid I may not recognize you when I see you again," he cried. "I hope you will still be as pretty as a pond lily."

After Julián left, the summer dances started. It was a happy time as the old men beat the drums and the women danced. "I would like to dance," María murmured, "but my baby is sick and I can't leave her." María carried the baby to the dances and watched the beautiful motion.

The women danced with a lift and a sweep as if their voices and movements would make a strong wind. The wind was supposed to sweep bad things away and bring in goodness. *I hope it blows away the bad,* María thought, snuggling her daughter close to her.

During the night the baby grew worse. María called her mother to help her. They bathed the baby to bring down her fever and fed her romerillo tea to drink. In spite of what they did the baby continued to grow worse.

"Mother, let's smoke her again," María begged. "It helped me when I had the spotted sickness. Maybe it will help her."

Mother shook her head. "No, María," she said, "it's too late. Pond Lily is dead."

They sent for the priest and made plans for burial. Usually they buried a baby under the floor of the storehouse so it could be at home with the family. "No!" cried María. "I can't bury my baby there and walk over her. Ask the priest if she can be buried in the church courtyard." The priest gave consent.

After her child died María sat on the front porch and looked at the old cottonwood tree. She missed Julián and the tree offered little comfort to her. It was a long, hard journey to reach Julián. It would be best to wait with this sad news. *I don't think that shadow ever moves an inch,* she thought, watching the long shadow it cast. *Time goes so slowly without Julián and the baby.*

Julián finally returned from the dig and María met him at the door. She began to sob. "Where's Pond Lily?" he asked.

"She's gone," María sobbed. "Right after you left for the dig." They clung to each other, crying. Afterwards Julián couldn't talk about his daughter.

"I think we should work very hard," María told him. "Maybe we can stop thinking about her so much." Lost in their work, they made pots for use in their kitchen and pots to sell. Yet when the tourist season started they had almost too much work. They found it difficult to fill all their orders.

"We must hurry," María said, helping Julián get ready to fire some pots one day. "They will be knocking on our door before we have these ready."

When they took the pots out they were dismayed. Three of them had turned black. "I wonder what happened," María remarked. "Maybe it's because the fire went out and they were smoked."

"Don't show them to anyone," Julián said. "Let's hide them." María hid the pots in the back of the storehouse and covered them with an old cloth.

Months later an archaeologist came to visit them. He wanted to buy pots. At the time they only had a few ready to sell. "Is this all you have?" he asked.

Because they needed money, María brought out the black ones. When the man saw them he became excited. He realized that they had rediscovered a lost art form of their ancestors, one that had been missing for over seven hundred years.

"Let's make lots of black pots," María said to Julián when they learned their value.

"Let's polish them with lard like Father does his saddles," Julián said. "It makes them shine."

Soon business was better than ever but tragedy struck again. María's mother died and left a baby girl for María to raise. She was María's baby sister, Clara. In the next few years María had four boys of her own to raise plus Clara. Later they all learned sign language as Clara became deaf from an illness.

Julián spent most of his time in the trading post selling their wares. He had learned to speak better English and could handle the sales. María was proud of Julián but she noticed his hands were beginning to tremble when he tried to paint. Once when he was coming up the hill she wondered what was wrong with him. She watched him stagger from side to side and when he opened the door he fell on his face.

He's been drinking wine again, María thought. *He's been to see the man who lives near the pueblo.* The man sold wine to Indians although it was illegal to do so. "I'll fix that," María murmured, as she tried to help Julián into bed. "I won't have Julián destroyed by white man's liquor."

While Julián slept she took Saint Joseph's picture off the wall and broke the plaster under it. She reached inside, pulled the money out, and placed it in her apron pocket. She hurried down the road to the man's house. "I want to buy your place," she said sternly.

His eyebrows shot up and he gasped. "I don't think you have enough money to buy it."

"How much?"

"Two thousand," he replied smugly.

María reached in her pocket and counted out the bills. "Now move," she said.

"I'll move as soon as I can," he said, pocketing the money. "Real soon."

"Not soon," María retorted with a glare. "Today!"

CHAPTER TEN

Julián

After the man moved away Julián changed. He worked hard. He began experimenting with new designs for the black pots.

"I'll grind and cook some guaco plant. It will make black paint for you to work with," María said.

Julián tried his new designs on a few polished pots. Then with his yucca brush he painted an avanyo, a plumed water serpent that had four humps on it. It represented the first rush of water coming down an arroyo. It was his symbol of thanksgiving for water and rain. It became his most famous design and created quite a stir.

While Julián decorated María's pots, he discovered how to put a matt (dull) painting on a polished surface. It was a simple technique he invented. He took a polished pot before it was fired and painted a design on it with red slip (a creamy mixture of red clay and water). The pot was then smoked black in the firing. He enjoyed decorating María's pots and his favorite design was the plumed water serpent.

It was a good time for María and Julián. María was proud of him. *He's a good husband,* she thought. *Even if he doesn't farm.*

One night Julián didn't come home. María expected

him back long before dark. She sat by the fire waiting for him as she darned his socks.

Perhaps he's gone to see someone in the pueblo, she thought anxiously. She waited all night and the next day, but still no Julián. She peered through the windows looking for him but it was no use. She noticed that the light snow had turned into a blizzard.

A strong wind roared through the pueblo. María shivered. She couldn't wait for him anymore. Exhausted she fell asleep on the bed.

A loud rap on the door awakened her. It was Adam. "Mother, get up," he said. "We found Julián."

"Where?"

"Some boys found him up behind the hill," he answered. "He must have gotten lost in the snowstorm."

"I want to see him," María said, grasping Adam's arm.

"He is dead, Mother. He froze to death."

María waited until the wagon returned with Julián's body. She pulled her shawl over her head and walked outside to the wagon. It was unusual for a woman to see her dead husband but María wanted to. *He looks so peaceful,* she thought. *Not at all tired.*

"Help us gather his personal things," Adam said. "You know we must destroy them."

"Aie," María responded with a nod, handing him Julián's favorite paintbrushes. She remembered when he had chewed the ends to make them soft. She could almost see his hand trembling as he painted her pots.

After collecting all his things the men took Julián deep into the mountains for burial. No one else knew where they buried him, not even María.

"I don't want to make pots anymore," María told Clara. "Not without Julián." She shut herself away and wouldn't leave the house. When anyone came near her house she hid and refused to answer the door.

One day a man caught her outside and asked to buy a

pot. "I don't have any," she said. "I don't make pots any- more." He pulled on his beaded gloves to leave and asked if he could come back later.

When María saw the gloves her eyes lit up. He gave the gloves to her and she invited him back. Later, when he came back, María sold him the last big pot she and Julián had made together.

That spring many cars poured into the pueblo with people looking for her pots. When she heard the crunch- ing of tires María grabbed her apron and motioned for Clara to follow. She decided she had been idle long enough.

"Come, Clara," she signed to her sister. "There is work to be done. We must get busy. We have pots to sell." She was eager to meet the public again.

Soon María was making pots and Clara polished them. Adam dug the clay and his wife, Santana, decorated them.

Later her son Popovi Da, "Po," worked with her. Po's enthusiasm and talent for making pots matched hers. Again, María laughed and sang, as working with Po became a special time in her life. It was said that during the fourteen years they worked together their work achieved a higher level of artistry.

When Po cleverly added the date to their pots, María laughed. She reminded him of her secret mark of identifi- cation in her pots. She had been marking them for a long time.

María had pressed her hand print in every pot she made. That way she always knew when a pot was hers. She signed her pots *María Poveka*. Those made with Po were signed *María / Popovi*.

"I think your work is like Julián's," she teased Po. Then she mischievously added, "But Julián's was better."

María and Popovi were invited to universities, where they made speeches and demonstrated their work. They kept busy with all these engagements. Wherever they went they traveled by station wagon. They took sand, clay, and even manure to fire the pots. María wanted their work to be authentic.

After Popovi became ill and died, Santana and Adam helped María with her pots. The family also continued to travel and demonstrate María's work. For convenience she and Clara moved in with Adam and Santana.

By then María had received so many awards that many were lost or forgotten. She was invited to the White House by five different presidents.

In 1968 she received the American Ceramic Society's Highest Award for Life Long Dedication to Clay. A short time later she was awarded a grant from the National Endowment for the Arts.

When Columbia College of Chicago presented her with an honorary doctorate degree, she didn't want to accept it. "I don't want to doctor," she said. "I want to make pots."

When the Smithsonian Institution held a retrospective show in Washington, D.C. in her honor, she knew she would see some of her old pots. On arrival, she greeted all her pots as she would her children or old friends. After greeting them, she slipped her hand inside to find her own hand print. When she checked out all the pots, she walked slowly to the podium with the aid of her stick cane.

Then peering over the top of her horn-rimmed glasses, she smiled shyly at her audience. She raised her hands and in Tewa gave a benediction that touched the crowd. She thanked Mother Earth, God, and all the people who bought her work.

When asked if she planned to do a lot of traveling to demonstrate her work she shook her head. "All I want to do," she said, "is make pots. I want to stay at the pueblo and help others.

"We should share," she added. "Pottery making belongs to the pueblo so everyone can have money." María did share. She shared her knowledge, her skill, and even her money. After that the financial level of the pueblo rose.

When guests came to their house, María rushed to her room and donned a purple dress and all her fine jewelry. Later, when she appeared at the top of the steps, she stood quietly waiting for Adam to introduce her. Always the clown, Adam would point his nose at María and say, "This is my mother . . . Phyllis Diller!"

CHAPTER ELEVEN

Letting Go

One day María said, "Adam, I'm tired. I don't want to make speeches or make pots anymore. I want to stay at home. I want to rest." However, it wasn't to be.

Day after day people poured into the pueblo. They wanted to see María. Some wanted to buy pots and others just came to look.

Even though María was weary, she kept a smile on her face. With the help of her stick cane she posed willingly when cameras began to click. It became a time of remembering. She liked to tell of all the famous people who came to see her. She loved telling of Lady Bird Johnson's visit.

"The secret service men came to the pueblo first. Oh . . . they were a joke," she recalled. "They told us to keep the children away from the First Lady. When Lady Bird arrived," she giggled, throwing her hand over her mouth, "she went straight for the children. She knelt on the ground, hugged them, and talked to each one."

María continued to say how nice Lady Bird and Eleanor Roosevelt were. She was invited to the White House by Mrs. Roosevelt several times. She visited Joan Mondale, too, whose husband was the vice-president of the United States at the time. The last pot she made was for Joan. She made it on the front porch. "Joan carried it all the way to Washington in her hand," she said, cupping her hand to show how she carried it. "And it wasn't even fired!"

In between visitors she liked to sit on the front porch thinking of days gone by. She dreamed of the time when she saw deer and buffalo come up over the hill early in the morning. Closing her eyes she thought of the cloudy mist that hung over the trees and bushes.

Most of all her thoughts turned to Julián and the sound of his voice. Her eyes followed the shadow of the old cottonwood tree. She remembered how slowly the shadow seemed to move while Julián was away when Pond Lily died.

But it seems longer now, she thought one evening, listening for the rustle of the tree's leaves. *Much longer.* Slowly she made her way to bed. She felt ill.

The next day Adam and Santana took María to the hospital in Santa Fe. María didn't like the hospital. "Please take me home, Adam," she begged. "I don't want to stay here."

The doctor agreed with María. He said because of her age there was nothing he could do for her. "It's best to take her home."

Clara sat by María's bedside all that day. She wouldn't leave, not even to eat. They had been more than sisters. They were like mother and daughter with a special blood tie. It was a close relationship that the pueblo respected.

"Clara, you must eat," Adam scolded. "I will stay here until you finish dinner." Clara ate her dinner and went back to María. She refused to leave María's side.

Late that night, July 20, 1980, María died. She died in her own bed at the pueblo, as she would have wanted. The women worked long into the night dressing her for burial. They used turquoise and sacred cornmeal for part of the preparations. Then they wrapped her in the traditional red blanket. What she had not given away before her death was destroyed. As was the custom, others in the family prepared food to serve after the funeral.

Early the next morning a mass was said for her at the church. Three priests from neighboring pueblos came to help Father Conran celebrate the mass. Near them stood a singer from San Juan Pueblo, softly beating a drum. In Tewa, María's beloved language, he sang "How Great Thou Art" and "Ave Maria."

After the songs Father Conran stepped forward and looked down at María's little form lying on the floor. "María," he said, "remember when you were a little girl and learned to make pottery? You never made a pot without praying to Mother Earth ... and thanking her. You didn't want to dishonor her by doing inferior work. You loved her, María." Father Conran paused. In almost a whisper, he added, "And now, María, Mother Earth has come for you. To enfold you in her arms ... to make you a part of her."

A few minutes later, María lay on the ground by her freshly dug grave. Still wrapped in the blanket, without casket or flowers, she was lowered into the loving arms of Mother Earth.